ALL THE WORDS I CAN REMEMBER ARE POEMS

ALSO BY MICHELLE PEÑALOZA

Former Possessions of the Spanish Empire
landscape / heartbreak

ALL THE WORDS I CAN REMEMBER ARE POEMS

Michelle Peñaloza

2024 LEXI RUDNITSKY EDITOR'S CHOICE AWARD WINNER

A Karen & Michael Braziller Book
PERSEA BOOKS / NEW YORK

The collages that appear throughout the book were created by the poet. More of her art can be found at michellepenloza.com.

PERSEA BOOKS, INC.
90 Broad Street
New York, New York 10004

LIBRARY OF CONGRESS CATALOGING-IN-PUBLICATION DATA

Names: Peñaloza, Michelle author
Title: All the words I can remember are poems / Michelle Peñaloza.
Description: First edition. | New York: Persea Books, 2025. | "A Karen & Michael Braziller Book" | Summary: "Winner of the 2024 Lexi Rudnitsky Editor's Choice Award and the James Laughlin Award from the Academy of American Poets, All The Words I Can Remember Are Poems challenges colonized ideas of history and truth, particularly in relation to Filipinx/a/o history and its colonization by the United States. Engaging with archival materials and playing with the sounds of remembered words and their unique associations, Michelle Peñaloza confronts violent and ironic tensions within historical narratives, subverting erasure and creating her own cultural fluency that speaks to growing up in diaspora and the complexities of identity, motherhood, and the transmission of love across generations"—Provided by publisher.
Identifiers: LCCN 2025016794 (print) | LCCN 2025016795 (ebook) | ISBN 9780892556274 paperback | ISBN 9780892556281 ebk
Subjects: LCGFT: Poetry
Classification: LCC PS3616.E525 A45 2025 (print) | LCC PS3616.E525 (ebook) | DDC 811/.6—dc23/eng/20250411
LC record available at https://lccn.loc.gov/2025016794
LC ebook record available at https://lccn.loc.gov/2025016795

Book design and composition by Rita Skingle
Typeset in Sabon Lt Pro
Manufactured in the United States of America.
Printed on acid-free paper.

JUDGES' CITATION FOR THE 2024 JAMES LAUGHLIN AWARD FROM THE ACADEMY OF AMERICAN POETS

Navigating humor and sorrow—and never neglecting the startling and subversive joy that can be found at their intersection—Michelle Peñaloza uses music and elegantly constructed moments of surprise to guide her reader with a seemingly effortless yet brilliantly deliberate hand. Transposing the mythologies and historical artifacts of an often buried Philippine history and the complex diasporic self-vision of a post-colonial Pinay daughter, Peñaloza's *All the Words I Can Remember Are Poems* is a sure-footed and confident second collection that establishes this poet's vision as distinct and unforgettable. These poems illuminate the expansive and specific perspective of a multilingual and multicultural speaker with playful precision and sophistication, utilizing modes and meanings that renew the power of storytelling. Here is an unapologetic voice, one that is not afraid to take up necessary space and to claim her belonging in the world, a voice that rings as clearly as a fiercely struck bell.

—TARFIA FAIZULLAH, KEETJE KUIPERS, AND BARBARA JANE REYES

Mga minahal, inibig. Lumisan, pumanaw—handog, alay sa inyo.

CONTENTS

I

II

III

I

Losing A Language

We were born with
a large door on our backs. When will
we know if it opens?

—VICTORIA CHANG

All The Words I Can Remember Are Poems

anak	like a sigh born every day
ilong	lead by scent and knowhow
tanong	asking questions about the world
sayaw	like how dance that comes from joy
sayang	can sway so close to sorrow
bayan	how shame could be an entire country
pinto	or an open-doored question
kailangan	needing, needful and needless
ilaw	illuminating a path
ikaw	to you, little bit of me, almost
dito	will you appear here
doon	are you still there, maybe
dahon	I hear you in the leaves
darating	rippling in the wind, always arriving

Why Not End This Experiment?

What can I offer my mother
when we cannot agree on the truth?
I send her flowers. I fill a digital Costco cart
with dehydrated shiitake mushrooms
and nuts she's not supposed to eat.
I ask her how she makes her misua.
She tells me church is safe. That everyone
wears a mask. That the Holy Spirit and
love of our Lord Jesus Christ keeps her
safe. What we don't say between *thank you*
and *upo* or *patola* and *I'm glad you are*
safe is a wound. I read somewhere
that imposter syndrome finds its roots
in childhood. That the emotional un-
availability of a child's caregivers makes
a child prove and prove again their
worth. I tell my mother my friend has died.
My friend who was like a mother. My mother
asks first: *Where?* I always fixate on how
she always finds the wrong thing to say.
As a child, I corrected her pronunciation
as she read me bedtime books.
In college, I confessed that memory to a white
professor, my shame rising to my face:
Isn't that messed up? Her blue eyes rolled,
exasperated—*You're so sentimental!*
All that means is you're a writer
and have been from the beginning!
I can't tell what the truth is from here.
Here are things I know: my titas hide
their cravings. Pretend they don't want
pigs' blood, that their mouths don't water
when I open a jar of bagoong. I know

my mother made a life for herself
despite always being the one
to kill what must be killed.

Barangay

We've met. We
rowed a long canoe
from one end of horizon
to another.

Waves

Outside the cemetery
two men beat one dog.
Nothing in this world is fair
fighting. My mother called
to say they found blood
in her sister's brain
they found cancer
in her sister's uterus
they found cancer
in her sister's lungs
so many to lose in a family
of twelve born
from the impossibility
of one woman's ability to
say no. *Yes* born from necessity
born from war. Is that why
prayer always provides
the safest balm?

When my mother prays
I don't.
I wonder instead
what she thanks invisible men for
then I stop. I know
what she is
(what I've never had to be)
thankful for—
a table once always empty
save for some patis over rice
now (Thanks Be to God)
gluts over with sugared ham,
well-done steak and creamed
casserole after casserole.

A dog cowers but
returns to his masters, eyes lowered
back flint to flinch.
Two men beat one dog.
It is what they can
beat. There's no beating
the holes in their pockets
or the nothing unfilled
by the needles they bring here.
The cemetery's decorated
with fake foliage and the leavings
of sharp relief. My mother keeps
long- scentless potpourri
and silk flowers
among her shrines
of blue-eyed Jesus, Santo Niño,
Mother Mary.

My tita is three hours into the future
her head open on a table.
What waves swell
in a bleeding brain?
We all have our ways
to anticipate. My mother prays
and I say I will, too
and together,
we wait.

I Tell My Mother I Don't Think Trying to Get Pregnant During a Pandemic Is a Good Idea

Everyone assumes we know how to love. Where
did you first learn? (Or did you ever)? In this blooming

a message: the bird which heals itself
is bandaged by an unseen hand. I asked

the earth to distill into one bone, into
the nadir of a mountain. I found buried there

my fear transformed into a jackrabbit
bounding away from me, an upside-down

heart moving across the Ouija board of this valley
reminding me that time is a floating island,

a menagerie of stars and crystals growing from children's
play lab kits and nautilus lisps—I asked: child

or no child—and the apple gave me the gift
of four seeds, perfect wisdom if not

wooden—what is the difference between
earth and terra? The landscape unfolds, unspools

like a soft plume. The chrysalis is a crossroads.
A fat grub born every minute. The air fat

with feathers in this ceremony of eternal candles.
La luna changes her mind often—child or no child

—blooming a new face, unraveled ligature
unbound and unbothered.

Kailangan

All the women
in my family
are needed
and needle
themselves into
whatever everyone
else needs.
No one ever
announces what
is needed,
which is nothing,
needless to say.

Inside My Lola's Handbag

a sandwich bag of chicken bones
a sandwich bag of tissues (used)
a palm-sized Santo Niño, Louis XIV Sun King
        (Skyflake crumbs and dust in his plastic hair)
Werther's Original wrappers
a sandwich bag of sandwich bags

How to Not Forget

Sweep. First with walis ting ting then with walis tambo. Thank the dust and dirt for giving you a moment of purpose. Brew a strong cup of coffee. Put a glass bottle of Coke in the fridge. Roll and smoke a joint. Put on Pilita, the one with the tattered cover: Pilita in a white terno, her eyes heavy with black liner, her hair a high, high bouffant. Admire how she rides an impressive kalabaw in front of a sad bahay kubo. Lay on the floor and say aloud the words you can translate in real time:

ganda *lungkot* *kahirapan* *puso* *buhay* *ginto*

Listen to your stomach: kumain ka ba? Crave a chili cheese hotdog. Curse being so far from a Coney Island or a Sonic. Remember the pork belly you bought from Costco; slice and sauté it with a knob of ginger, a whole bulb of garlic, and a fistful of sili. Bagoong to taste. Coconut milk. Simmer. Pour it all over a clean bed of steaming Cal Rose. Eat until your heart feels less empty. Cry. Don't cry. All your ghosts get it. They miss you, too. Take that cold Coke out of the fridge. Hold the glass to your third eye. Try to remember that story about Francis Ford Coppola bringing a truck of Coca-Cola for the whole barangay, everyone an extra in the zenith of his opus, an imperialist remix of an imperialist text, paid in sugar and caffeine. Didn't the dictator let the director borrow a fleet of helicopters? Think about the rhyme of *flame* and *fame*. Think of that poet who left cans of Coke and notes that began . . . *is even more fun than going to San Sebastian.* Shrug to your ghosts—What? You never slept with him. Enjoy your burn of bubbles. Burp. Recall of all the ghosts you carry in your body. Gather all the mirrors in your home, a piece of broken capiz; the calamansi juice, pandan leaves, banana leaves solidified in your freezer (you can't get fresh, but you can get frozen two hours from where you live). Wrap yourself in the hot pink malong you bought in Quiapo and memorize a menu comprised of at least twelve desserts. Light all the purple candles in the house. Make promises. Sabihin mo lahat dito sa Tagalog, sabihin mo laging malungkot ka pagkatapos sabihin mo hindi laging totoo yan. Sabihin mo kailangan pa kita, sabihin mo marami ka pang gagawin. Sabihin mo hindi mo alam kung tama 'to and hope that your ghosts forgive you for your clunky tongue, for all you keep trying to remember.

What You Remember When You and Your Mother Say Miss You Back and Forth on the Phone After Not Having Seen Each Other in Person for Almost Two Years

winter made the dark
        come on quicker

        you are three, maybe four
still small enough to hide   still fearful of your mother
not in sight

        there is a circle of light
above you   a halo made
        by this place you have chosen
            to hide
the sad carpet
        of middle America
is now your bed
                this circle is now your home

purple wool   red nylon   black faux fur
fuchsia   brown   navy
cashmere   mohair   cotton

this wheel of hanging coats
                covers you like the willow tree
in front of your house
                another place you also hide

an hour ago your learned
        ES
            CA
                LA
                    TOR
made your mother teach you

AG AIN
AG
AIN
ES
CA
LA
TOR

AG
AIN
the floor below eating the very earth

ES
CA
LA
LA
LA
LA
LA
LA
LA
until finally your mother

ferried you off the black river

LA TOR

now from your nest
you hear other mothers
(not your mother) with other children (not you)
the back and forth of command
and exasperation
you have

triumphantly escaped

except

your victory

frightens you

your poor mother she is also lost

without you

My Mother and Her Sisters Scream When They See Snakes (Even on TV)

It's not that I am unafraid, more that
their fear is red-hot and prickled

where mine feels more like the wind—
a rising flare in my nostrils as I inhale and ex-

hale in time with the movements of a creature
so unlike me—no legs, no arms, no hair, no warmth.

My mother and her sisters have lived many
lives different than mine, in places with fear woven

into everything: the nipa roof, the snakes sa ilog
as dangerous as the Devil or the long glossal hunger

of the manananggal whose hunger might scrape
a baby brother from your mother's womb.

And what of the dictator, the gross boss, the leering
kuya impossible to avoid? I suppose we, like all women,

have them in common, these men crawling on their bellies,
flicking their tongues to convince us what's best.

Still, how close have any of them come to an actual snake?

Before I left the city, I'd spotted a garter or two.
Maybe coyly pet a boa constrictor on some school trip to the zoo.

But here, among our newly planted green rows each spring,
I mark the snakes' paths by smell alone. A smell like a whole

school of fish swimming in earth instead of ocean,
with a hint of what I can only name as eyelash glue.

This summer was one of so many snakes—
under the un-deadheaded dahlias, attempting

for so many feet to unsuccessfully slither
through the chicken wire; diving down

what I had thought was a gopher hole; a quick
em dash between the compost piles

—and though they startle me each time, my heart
shot straight up to my gullet, I remember

real snakes mean you have a healthy garden,
mean the apple is not far behind.

Kalokohan

My friend's kid discovers the glory of Gloria Estefan and, when prompted by her mother's question, "Is the rhythm gonna get you?" declares, "DON'T TALK ABOUT IT!" as she waves her small arms high above her head.

If you plant one clove of garlic, it will grow into a bulb. If you plant one zucchini a summer, it will be enough.

When he wasn't working at the plant or working in his garden, my father wore his Florsheim loafers and took care to condition their black leather and make their small gold buckles shine.

My mother giggles high-pitched, like a little girl with her eyes-skyward when she tries to tell a story, so funny, so funny she can't catch her breath. I laugh, too—her laughter contagious, "So, what happened? What happened?"—until my cheeks hurt, though I haven't yet heard a plot or punchline.

Once I hiked through a jungle and climbed to the summit of a mountain and there found every houseplant my parents placed throughout the corners of my childhood: pothos, snake plant, rubber tree, purple queen, ficus, fern. *Indoor, outdoor; outdoor, in.*

A robin wakes me three mornings in a row with a BANG BANG BANG that chokes me from my sleep: its poor beak, trying to break through the windows. No, no, I say. You will hurt yourself. That reflection is you. There is no other robin here. Just you, just you. I rush the window. Raise my arms, make myself big to scare it away from itself. A monster trying to help.

Attempts at Order

Allora, buys you a little time for the throat-clearing,
before boredom or a butterfly or the business of dailyness
creeps into the art you've been trying to render into something before
dinner must be made. Too late. You've launched into a poem:
expectations have been set, like in school: A is always better than—
forget this! You're interested in parameters but your dead, your loving
ghosts keep returning to test and test again your various boundaries.
Helicoptering over your head, indivisible and impatient.
Immigrants all carry ghosts like balloons ready to pop in
July heat, though some are good at ignoring the squeak of rubber.
Kitchen ghosts are common and predominant in your family—
lamenting in the rice cooker, chuckling in the chicken bones. Your
mother rarely spends time in the kitchen, the older she gets.
No one asks her to cook anymore. Her tongue: heavy and beautiful.
Opal is her birthstone—pale and shining, both hot and cold—
parameters of fire and ice in one gem. Your mother no longer
questions aloud the decisions you've made. In your older ages, she's
resigned (it seems) to the fact of how her daughter (you)
sails through the world. Not often, in fact, never unless you
transform the informal idiom, taking into account how
unglamorous and actually difficult sailing must be—it looks
very hard, doesn't it? You've never been a great swimmer.
What wisdom can be wrangled from your failures? Oh, to
X-ray your mistakes for some kind of lesson—yes, that'd be useful.
Yet, there's still remembering and forgetting, zigging and
zagging toward some ideal, toward some order that makes sense.

Zodiac

I am a Pig, the placemats tell me, blessed
with a beautiful personality and good fortune.
Compatible with Tigers, Rabbits, and Goats.
The first time I went to a pig farm
was also the first time I met my dead father's
dead brother's daughters. My cousins,
who owned and ran a piggery.
I was twelve. My father was not yet dead.
Theirs was. Slaughtered by a shower
of bullets sprayed into the side of his car.
A Hyundai Starex become a perforated night sky.
Their brother, my cousin, was slaughtered, too.
So much dead family I'll never meet.
According to myth, the Pig arrived
last for the emperor's great meeting
and so was named twelfth, the very last in the Zodiac.
My father was one of eleven, the last boy
to arrive in the family, just after his brother,
my slaughtered uncle. At the farm, I saw
the mammoth girth of a full-grown sow,
heavy with a drift of piglets.
Later, in honor of my father's homecoming
some twenty-five years after he left
the rusty country, left the piggery,
left the cigarette smoke in the funeral parlor,
seven years after his brother's murder,
we all ate a whole lechon—no part wasted,
the skin remarkably crisp
from hours of a fattened animal
having done the economical work
of basting itself on a spit.

Pagdadalamhati

the salt thrown over the shoulder
the sand a child insists will subdue the ocean
the halving and halving of atoms
that births inexplicably
a new thing—halved
and halved in our no longer having
you nor you nor you nor you
no longer you never
again you

Hangang Sa Muli

We see our dead everywhere.
A butterfly, a bat—*Lola? Dad?*
Is that you? Just today,
I saw my father in the long
finger of an okra, overgrown past
peak deliciousness. It waggled at me—
naku, not even good for deep-frying!—
and reminded: tingnan mo! Always
look close at your garden, at your hands,
at the layers of dust and corner cobwebs
gathered in the spaces you pass
each day—there! I am there, I am
here. Always beside you. Always
swirling around you, inside you.
Only one breath away.

Kalungkutan

makes reckless cosmologists of us all
and so we build new gods and universes,
strike bargains for epic consequences:
if I find that old notebook, I will not have
lost my memories of you; if I still manage
to keep safe the note you wrote me four-
teen years ago, it will mean I can keep you
here. If I walk into the world, looking for
you around each corner, one day
you will appear.

II.

[W]ord-subversion, however unconsciously, has always been a way to poke at power. E.g., the colonizer, contrarily, is hyper-un-aware. The colonized, by her multiplicity, is always a step ahead—like a writer.

—GINA APOSTOL

A fair maiden of Manila, Philippine Islands

Stereograph: School Girl in Native Dress, Upper Garment Made of Hemp Gauze, Philippine Islands, 1907.

To be a pupil of household industries: what it means to be a proper wife: the meaning they give me. I sit with my embroidery. They enter with great fanfare. Direct me to sit here. They say *docile* to each other and not to me, thinking I will not know such a word. Their words: *Native maid.* I know them: blank, dense hunger. I stare straight at their want, exuding the equanimity of an alien flower. I watch their shoes, wool and whisker of them, hairy shuffle, bidding me to be as still as possibility. I set myself to rigor as they disappear behind the camera, beneath the cloth. I hold a closed fan in my hands, which hold all my wishes to slap these men, strike this fan across their faces. When they shoo me away, I leave my broken fan, twice.

Continental Drift

What does it say that we come from an ocean
people, surrounded by water, and none of us
really knows how to swim? I know how to not
drown, but can't swing a stroke, only paddle.
A dog fetching my breath further and further
from my hot mouth. And what of floating on
the surface? Age has made me increasingly
sick on the ocean more than once—what
would my ancestors make of my weakness,
my inability to hold the horizon's movements
in balance, this propensity for vertigo? Bakit,
anak? I have no answer for how we travelled
so far there's no going back. I am a landlubber,
a child of cars driving past acres of corn and tobacco.
I walk through fields of wheat, rippling a golden sea.

Stereograph: The Bones of the Tenants Whose Burial Rental Was Not Renewed—Santa Cruz Cemetary, Manila, 1899

skull skull femur *they inspect us* radius ulna *bundok na buto* tibia *puzzles* skull sacrum *inscrutable alive* scapula coccyx *perhaps solvable dead* humerus clavicle mandible *a problem of tenancy* skull sternum *can our* femur skull *bones pay anything forward* rib skull rib tibia *could our hauntings* femur tibia mandible *be monetized* pubis ilium *these two fools* skull ischium *are not princes* tarsus skull patella *and not one of us a jester* vertebra tibia skull skull skull *or momento mori* fibula tibia femur *but occupancy manifest* skull pubis mandile *we have yet to return to dust* clavicle scapula *where our eyes once were* humerus skull sacrum skull *we can still gape back* femur mandible vertebra *into their empty gaze* skull sternum skull *no way to desecrate us* tibia scapula femur *further* tarsus skull skull skull skull skull skull skull

Inventory

femur back oxtail chicken pig milkfish tinik buto smooth jagged stones river stones
stones skipping rivers dagat koi ponds backyard ponds
creeks culverts lakes falls full
water lettuce waterlilies banana leaves halaman acacia hyacinth roses red
roses yellow magnolia balete cattails
crape myrtle nipa Bradford pear bougainvillea dogwood palm
bromeliad puno
puso bangus dilis lionfish milkfish clownfish angelfish ocean fish
gold fish river fish swimming without knowing
how to lungoy
funeral parlors karaoke sa sala cockfights drunk fights full flights
bahala na sa buhay mo cigarette smoke
cherry kept close to the throat
houses on stilts on a lake
inside a volcano inside a lake on an island of many islands
in an ocean of oceans golden lobes golden piercings Cadillac gold chains
golden globs of injection molding UAW card carrying
Big Three paychecks Big Three pink slips muscle cars carrying car seats
salt and snow
twenty to a five-room suburban sidewalks subsumed by the
smell of frying fish
Romulus without Remus born dear
from toddler-sized boxes filled here opened there boxes bound back
by tape and rope
holding in Tommy and Ralph and Nike and Hershey and Spam
only there atis sukang paombong chico alamang maliit
mga mukha not strangers until magsalita or ngiti
further back
a bangka an ark islands two by two
4000 kinds of orchids dito doon

Stereograph: After a Typhoon—Wherever the Roof Lands, There the Filipino Makes His Home, 1912

All they can see through their little boxes: *home*, removed twice. Indio. Filipino. Double-double. Any fool knows a roof intact is no miracle, but a blessing of design. What do they know of God's Eye? Blinks of mercy between rain, of bayanihan? These 'kano know nothing about kababayan nor any true need to recreate. We know you don't pour foundations in cement, but in the many arms come together to move a house: a choice. We know the importance of know-how: how to build many homes not your own, how to ask for nothing. Bubong. Silid. Silong. A music in the common sense of our homes. We know this land always provides—kawayan, nipa, kahoy, dahon—what we need to rebuild again and again and again and again and again and again and again and again and again and again and again and again

Keystone V

Pikon

translucent   onion skin
paper skirt
          whatever hurts
incurred   uncured
curdles like wasps
unfurled from a carcass
the meat beats
below the dermis

Standardization

Empire : Diaspora

a) Pollen : Capitalists
b) Gold : Honeybees
c) Loose Change : Chumps
d) Diaspora : Empire

Pamilya : Family

a) Love : Obligation
b) Boundary : Guilt
c) Obligation : Love
d) Distance : Regret

Utang na Loob : American Dream

a) Uncle Sam : Little Brown Brother
b) Province : Makati
c) Buhay : Patay
d) Typhoon : The Red Cross

Nanay: Anak

a) Bulaklak: Araw
b) Filipino : American
c) Hungry : Full
d) Anak : Nanay

Stereograph: 24045—American Soldiers Feeding Filipino Children

Pale men turn more and more red: poor contests losing their ideals. *They* are better? They kill our parents, pen us like piglets. Opportunities—little and probable brown bouts of power, born from ghost hands' appetite for glory. Look there, humanitarian! They think we will not bite. How wrong. Brown mouths, hungry, will grow up into scouts, great loud cogs, men & women spouting lingua franca, gratitude. Whitening, brightening as bettering as what's best. Ha! Free from weak blistered skin, we hold our truths: they know not one true thing of our ripening: a prize of unknown consequence. Their sport: which child hungers most? Starving in open lack, perfect photographs. Lo, progress! Mores doled, old feeding, roved emptiness, empty promise: empire's feed of benevolent assimilation. Primacy a dumb lie under our powerful crossing—these stupid lines, dirt pens whose contents will fatten, spatter so pleasing, so *salamat po*. They don't know how well we know to grow candor in the dark. Downcast our eyes: bundok dugo ngipin dilim. Our fresh gums, our red teeth.

Mga Manananggal Speak

i was one of the first
bruja *babaylan* they spit *aswang* *manananggal*
they made into a monster
they split me in two so I grew wings flew

the moon sang to my tongue
grow and grow
and grow and grow

beneath vestments beneath uniforms
they were just men
i slid beneath their mosquito nets
and slit their throats with my long razor
tongue
their blood tasted no different from any pig's

one day shame began stopping women
in the palengke
from embracing me
even after i'd healed their scars
after aborting what they could not
say no to
what they could not
afford to feed

my tongue already sharp
shrewd as my mind
my appetite whet for freedom
from my father's roof

my brother's watch
my neighbor's touch
my mother's lot

birò: *what's better—*
a woman's upper or lower half?

ask a Spanish friar *ask a Worcester*
ask a Lansdale *ask a Roosevelt*
ask the many sons of empire

our lower halves if found unattended
well, you know what they did

my cleaving : a relief
a great power
to no longer carry fruit
to no longer
swell in violation

i grow wings my tongue unzips

i am wolf i am owl i am bat i am mist

split rift drip slurp worm
gift need relief
i leave behind half of me

i don't walk

i fly

California

Gophers track sink holes all the way to your front door.
Unintentional moat. Keeping what out, keeping what in?
My mother believes *we were not ready*. Does she believe
in the camps? The price for insurrection, for unwillingness
to enact burden. Burden placed as yoke (a word I first learned
from the Oregon Trail): a device for the neck of the defeated.
An integral part of manifesting destiny. Joining animals,
joining shoulders to carry a load. Every day is a truck
driving through an ancient forest knocking down trees
that take 400 years to grow. Is that how my mother feels
when I call her, angry about the world? She's a survivor.
A master of alignment. Better: the lines she knows than
ones she would never draw. Every day is a truck driving
through an emptying field. Blood makes the grass grow tall.

The Bureau of Land Management Votes to Slaughter 44,000 Wild Horses to Make Room for Beef Cattle

the headline makes me think of being ten and the wind blows so hard across the valley
that PG&E cuts our power at midnight to save us from the risk of fire that's only a risk
because of PG&E power lines and the wind squeaks against the windows like a sound
quail make and I always wonder when I watch them fly—what it must feel like to fly
but so clumsily, a little football instead of a bird, the way loons seem more like wooden
toys trying to fly instead of the birds they actually are and I've been thinking I should
give up red meat, maybe meat altogether, and I wonder what will they do with those
horses and how many horses we can still call wild and how might you quantify or even
find wildness anymore especially if you grew up where the overall and underall ethos
was one of tameness by way of sameness and shame and fences and home theaters
in basements with built-in speakers and lawns and faux stone walkways and shade-
loving hostas and the accumulation of conveniences and hospitalities so potent as to be
effective and attractive stucco over bloody and terrible and tiresome things that seem
more like good things instead of the terrible that they are.

The Captions Are Handwritten

Insurgent prisoners guarded by American soldiers bearing insurgent dead. North of Malinta, Bulacan Province—1899.

> In an unplanted rice field, each insurgent prisoner holds a shovel. One soldier holds nothing, another leans on his rifle, another sits in the foreground.

A soldier is a person who serves in an army. To soldier (on) is to persevere.

> A soldier leans forward, his legs a legible figure four; his elbow meets his knee as his sneer meets the camera, as if he might say, "Why take a picture of this?" A few feet from his feet, an insurgent dead's hat sits intact, a few feet from his faceless head.

Insurgent prisoners are prisoners rising in active revolt who have been caught. Insurgent dead are dead people in active revolt.

> The crown of the dead insurgent forms an eye that meets the camera's gaze. His torso bloats taut. His hands make no sense relative to the location of his head and his feet.

The etymology of insurgent is "into, towards" and "to rise."

> The photograph's handwritten caption seems to hold a sad pun. Did the writer consider the wide differences between enduring and deliberately forgetting?

Writers seem to utilize etymology when they are at a loss for words, as if the origin of a word will provide more meaning.

> One can *bear* burdens, fruit, a hand, someone ill will, someone malice, a relationship to, a resemblance to, the stamp of, witness to. One can bear away, bear down, bear in on, bear off, bear on, bear out, bear up, bear with. One can not bear to think.

What did the writer of this caption know about language, about puns?

The same soldiers who rounded up and drove Indians onto reservations are the same soldiers who drove Filipinos into reconcentration camps. To bear the burden of massacre twice over, what do you think you must bury? Maybe that is the wrong question: can you bury a burden if it is named service?

The U.S. invented and perfected the "water cure" and psych warfare in the Philippines.

The passage of time, the shifting of context reflects the nuances of language. Take, "squatter" and "pioneer." "Colony" and "territory." "Subject" and "citizen." "Amigo" and "insurrecto." One can hear nuance in tone: "So, where are you from?" and "Yeah, where are you from?"

Is this caption proof a perpetrator can access sympathy—even empathy?—in subconscious slippage? Does this line of questioning ring in the register of wistful revision?

Every one of the U.S. Army's first twelve chiefs of staff served in the Philippine War.

The University of Michigan owns 2,141 photographs in an archive—*The United States and its Territories 1870–1925: The Age of Imperialism*—which features many photographs and stereographs (so you can see twice and with the right equipment in primitive 3D) of dead Filipinos in rice paddies and dirt trenches.

I've been down the rabbit hole of this archive many times.

There is a photograph: an enormous trench filled with dead Filipino men, women, and children. American soldiers stand over them, surveying the landscape as if they looked into a river of water instead of a valley of corpses. Four years after Roosevelt proclaimed the Philippine "insurrection" over: the Bud Dajo Massacre. W.E.B Du Bois displayed the photograph in his classroom to impress upon his students what "Wars of

Conquest really mean" and called the photograph "the most illuminating thing [he had] ever seen."

You may have noticed I, the poet, have introduced myself into this piece.

The negative of the photograph of "Battle of Bud Dajo" was "accidentally" destroyed by an unnamed American official.

After the war in Afghanistan, the Philippine American War is the longest one the U.S. has ever fought.

The breadth of records of a war that the whole of my American education failed to mention—a war I only learned about as an adult, a war with reconcentration camps in both of my parents' home provinces, a war in which it's estimated 775,000 Filipinos were killed—I find particularly fascinating.

I am a consequence of conquest.

An archaic definition of "fascinate" applies especially to snakes: to deprive a person or animal of the ability to resist or escape by the power of a look or gaze.

Reader, what is it I need you to know?

You, too, are a consequence of conquest.

We've been American for a very long time.

American Stereoscopic Company
Manufacturers and Publishers.
New York, N. Y. U. S.
725-727 Broadway.
Dead Filipino on the Battlefield near Malabon, Philippine Islands.
Copyright 1899 by R. Y. Young.

III.

Bawat katagang naihahabi ko sa tula
ay dulot mo

—ROFEL G. BRION

Utang Na Loob

It is the last day of the year and I am resolved
to write you the poem I owe you, the one we said
we'd write for the other the last time we met
well before The Before Times in the town
where they filmed *Murder, She Wrote.*
We walked through succulent gardens, heath, heather,
rhododendron, and dahlia all prospering in July heat,
to reach a room carved into the side of a cliff.
Inside: a gray whale-hip replica, a window overlooking
an ocean crevasse, and a scrappy display of various lichen,
a catalog of their names barely readable beneath cloudy glass.
Poets, we began to read them aloud—*blistered navel, firedot,*
giant shield, reindeer, witch's hair—such delight in taxonomy!
For years since we've taken turns remembering—
ah, I still owe you that lichen poem! Doesn't that prompt feel
so long ago? Finding delight, writing poems—
lately as hard as the consensus of what we all owe one another.
Last week, I hosted a second year of Christmas Zoom:
my cousin's kid quarantined in a separate square,
while my other cousin said everyone should just try
to get it and spread it so we can all get back to normal
to which my cousin whose son had been alone
in the basement for ten days waved his two middle fingers
at the camera and disappeared from the frame
and I laughed because of all the wine I drank
to be on that call and said *Merry Christmas, everyone!*
Every day I think of Gayia and Ged, their Zoom memorials
coordinated across time in Manila, Nashville, LA, and Honolulu,
how my ates would be absolutely alive had they the medicine
that half the people in this country refuse, how six million
people across the world are dead. Still, I owe you a poem
about lichens. They seem like single organisms, but really,
are two: a fungus, an alga—layered and inseparable.

Whether their relationship is mutualistic or parasitic, scientists
disagree. Whatever side you're on, it's true that lichens absorb
everything in their environment into their structure.
You are where you are. The last time I saw you, I met your sons.
We walked along the rocky shore that met the ocean
and regarded with care all the life we saw, your sons naming
—*mussel, limpet, anemone, starfish, barnacle*—all crammed
in their cold water, all waiting for the tide to come in.

Para Kay Tito Rofel, the First Poet in Our Family

Your life made mine possible—one of letters,
travel, love of language, food, tsimis and kwento
about our family—not that we can travel now,
nor do I send letters from Mendocino to San Pablo
nor are you my father. But you keep him. Knew him.
Loved him. You help me keep his memory, his love,
in this world. As a fellow poet, you might've noticed
how many times I've used the word *love*. I mean to
because this poem is for you. Ang pinaka-una sa
aming pamilya: how much love did it take to be
the first, to share and find love in so many countries?
Ilang puso? Sa pagtaas ng iyong kilay, I learned
kababayan at kapwa. I learned kalayaan
in the long reach of your laughter, sa iyong pag-ibig.

Inspiration

Maxine Hong Kingston
says she writes haiku daily.
She's, like, the best muse.

Doppelgänger

It upsets my tita
that people think she
looks like Oprah. She says
she wants to be a queen
in her own right. I think
it's more likely she is
racist. Or maybe she doesn't
want the rest of us to expect
a car (!) and a car (!) and a car (!).
Or maybe my tita is tired
of being a savior and a myth.

Huwag Kang Matakot

My tita texts me a picture
of a t-shirt that reads
You Can't Scare Me
My Wife Is Filipino.
A mid-flap Filipino flag frames
You Can't Scare Me My Wife Is
while a cartoon machete punctuates
the oversized punchline
FILIPINO!
My tita texts to ask if I want one
for my white husband
and for a moment I picture him
as one of the white men at Fil-Am BBQs
Oh no, I'll just stick to the lumpia
getting sunburned and drinking Coors
whispering to his wife to tell her friends
to only speak English when he's around
and I hold down the HAHA button on
my tita's text, my laughter bubbling blue
next to her question and I reply
I don't think he'd wear it, but
thank you! And I don't write
but I think about all the times I've
heard her say *We're not Filipino,*
we're American and how many times I've been
asked when I came to America and what it means
for the whole of your life to be determined
by having been born in one place and not
the other and my tita replies *OK everyone else*
wanted one and I don't know if she means
my other titas each wanted one for their
white husbands too or if the white men
they married, my uncles, each wanted one

for themselves, but the more I think about it
the more I think about what a woman might
want a machete for: clearing a path
of balete roots, scaling fish,
opening a coconut.

Failed Self-Portraits

as Last Cigarette
as Claudia Kishi
as Half-Eaten Baguette
as Drunk Bumblebee
as Cowboy Boots
as Bamboo Shoots
as Plastic Adirondack Chair
as Never Shoulda Been Permed Hair
as Telenovela Translation
as Nope Wrong Asian
as 90s Girl Group R&B
as Little Falling Butiki

Deals Only We Only Got Deals

I say, upon hearing the name, *imma write*
a poem with that title, the name of a store,
mentioned with specific regularity given how much
we all love deals as Jane tells us again how
its aisles are where Dollar Store finds go to die again,
further and faster than one can sing
Grocery Outlet, Bargain Market—
        Wait, so what exactly do they sell there?
Where is this place? How good are these deals?
        Is it stuff you actually wanna buy?
—questions erupt from all of our little Zoom boxes,
the moons of our faces reflecting one another's shine.
This is a Brady Bunch screen of badasses who've been
writing and painting and teaching and making
for decades, creators of so much content considered
too niche for so long it's now in demand, especially
upon viral terror and during specific months of the year
though right here and now
violence   *diaspora*   *grief*   *colonialism*
        misogyny   *racism*   *orientalism*   *imperialism*
are key words that don't enter this digital room.
Instead, we discuss if nail polish can actually go bad,
and speculate on more deals to be had
in a store with such a confident moniker.
Devon says, *I gotta see the sign for this place*
and Tessa drops a link in the chat
we all click to see, as Arlene says, *Ohhhhh*
        it's DEALS ONLY WE ONLY HAVE *DEALS*
and then we discuss how much better *got* functions than *have*,
how it feels more like access than possession,
and rings more assertive relative to the quality of said deals,
and, sonically, sounds much better, with the emphasis on
the more pleasing syllables—DEALS ONLY WE ONLY *GOT* DEALS

—we mutter and exclaim at varying speed and rhythm
the cadences of which I repeat under my breath
when in a sleepy Oregon town I finally find one
alone; I snap the signage and several aisles—
loofah poofs and rolls of masking, duct, electrical,
gaffer's, painter's and packing tape, a shelf of Batman and Joker
wrapping paper—and immediately begin a thread:

Yoooooo—this place is truly one immigrants and
children of immigrants can fully embrace and understand!

To which my phone bubbles over with hearts and hahas
and exclamations. There is so much I never want
to explain and feel bad bringing up but can't help
but reach out because I don't want to be alone
when I know I am not crazy but need someone to tell me I am not crazy
when someone attacks another auntie
when I brace myself for the news whenever I get texts like

Hey thinking of you and sending extra love

and so I am glad that when I sent extra love
to our group text, Arlene replied with a selfie:
her astonished face and a maxi pad
held beside her head to reference scale—
this maxi pad is FUCKING HUGE in its wrapping, already
so ridiculous—then she sends another image, the pad, now unfolded,
runs parallel from her raised eyebrows to her shoulders!
Can I even say how much I love us?
How, when the world is trash, there's trash pizza.
There's raccoon memes. There's real deal strategy for *The Floor is Lava*
and Supermarket Sweep. There's an SUV full of houseplants,
a Google Doc of where and when we'll eat corndogs,
an always available air mattress.
There's a wall of machetes,
an endcap of wooden canes and old nail polish,
a window display of garden gnomes bearing Canadian flags

beside discount bedpans, walkers, and crutches.
There's Arlene writing:
I will now envision absorbing
all the world's hatreds and horrors
into this magical x-tra absorbency shield
and throw it into the sun!
I will not explain.
Some deals only we get.
Only for us.

Babae

after the work of Goldie Poblador

ylang ylang blooms
only at night
petals the color and
shape of langka

in scent we develop
memory
longstanding intimacies

remember department stores
the giant bottles of perfume
glass on glass
festooned with gold

scent is a rhyme
of history
and momentum

ilang-ilang
ulam ulan
walang anuman

flower of flowers
            make a meal of rain
you're welcome

to this petal
this glass
this future this past

plucked at sunrise
it signals to moths and bats

come! come!

we'll inhale
imagined futures
together

楂餅
HAW FLAKES
山楂餅

Just Saying

I'm sorry I ate all the beef jerky. I know you wanted some. But I ate it all. It was salty and chewy and delicious. You make fun of me for turning everything into a poem. Farming's taught me how hard it is to actually turn anything that runs on a gas motor. The ditch witch and the rototiller pull you forward and only in the direction you choose to go first. A pull in only one direction is what I feel most these days, why I stuff my face with beef jerky—we've sunk our money into the ground, hoping what grows will turn into money and that money will turn into the life we're trying to grow. Calm down, I don't know if I'm talking kids. But I am trying to talk about something. Something like *abundance*, which comes from Latin, *abundantia*, meaning overflowing, like the way you fill our cups with water each night and place them on our nightstands. Because we need to stay hydrated. I'm always wanting and needing so much. Can need be over-flowing? Can need brim over? I'm sure there's something here I could relate to farming, how it's not about transformation so much as moving mass—pallets of dirt, buckets of compost tea—from one place to another, the wheelbarrow always in use, never resting, full of seabird pellets, with so much depending not upon it but on the strength or weakness of our arms on any given day. These days, I don't write anything down. But I listen. I actually hear the sound wings make when birds fly! What else could be more like a poem? Maybe that face you made when I did not answer when you asked, "What happened to all the beef jerky?"

Portrait at 38

after Kamilah Aisha Moon

My calamansi (try #2)
teases me: fragrant white flowers
then tiny green spheres
that stay and stay
tiny for weeks and weeks.
So many, nothing doing.
More sun? More water?

This year: unending
anticipation. I write, anak,
hoping to reach you,
my ancestor
yet to be born.

I picture you atop my father's shoulders.
At Lola's table, popping rice
into your happy mouth. I see you
running fast beside Ate Ged,
whispering a funny secret to Ate Gayia.
There you are, drawing an orange sun
onto white paper, Ate Susan looking on.

Where are we before
we are here, if not with those
who were here before with us?

I hope so much for you
to join us.

See, I can't even write
my own portrait without you in it?
Anak, picture me:

a curtain of black hair
I sometimes choose to hide behind.
The same thin lips as your lolo,
given to open wide in laughter.
This Peñaloza chin you will have, too,
softening with the softening
of all of me, preparing
for your arrival.

Spawn

Apply a question of love
to a dying salmon
guided back to the place
of its birth so its death
may provide for new life.
A very Catholic approach.
Here, in the forest
a smell of violets
beneath the rain. A bird
screeches as though
it says *breach breach*
at my appearance the sound
more like a scraping than a call.
I picture you miles away
transplanting new life
into the ground as I
seep for another month—
no baby, no seed, no life
in this blood. The last supper

we ate together before I left:
grilled salmon, its fat belly
and crisp skin delicious
with smashed cucumbers and
white rice sprinkled with furikake.
You had just emptied your kiln—
vessel after vessel, Crock Blue,
well-formed and unbroken.
The doctors have said it's
not you, but haven't
yet found
what is wrong
with me.

Updates

The alstroemeria last the whole month

The fire takes an hour to burn with enough heat

The rice cooker needs five more minutes

There might not ever be a baby

Q&A

What is the color of bruises?

> The needles, the endless tests—how many eggs left? How much time left?

What is the color of bruises?

> Strong enough to mark, not sharp enough to cut.

What is the color of bruises?

> My blame for time, for time's fits. The repetition of outrage, exhaustion, apathy, guilt—blooming on your skin, your heart. The heart is a muscle, vulnerable to contusion, to mar and mark. Everyday another rupture. Impact.

What is the color of bruises?

> The gutted fish, the fish's gills ribboned with smiles—how to breathe where you are ill-quipped? How to swim outside of water once you have discovered you can leave it?

What is the color of bruises?

> What seeps between my legs each month you are not born. Hindi buo. My sadness. My sliver of relief. My blame: choosing myself first, choosing you later, maybe, choosing you too late.

What is the color of bruises?

> A salt water fish in a red room. A wall of bright cookies. The inside of a tree. A garage full of birthday party, streamers and high chairs. A procrastinating cavity.

What is the color of bruises?

> My mother's roses—peach, yellow, lavender—a blooming perpetual, bordering a house, bordered by suburbia, bordered by hedges and fences and fear, bordered by history, bordered by continental flight, bordered by archipelago, bordered by hunger, bordered by so much need to survive.

Little One

little ant
little blade, little blueberry bunso
little cat
little dawn, little dark-haired diwa
little ear of little corn
little frigate, little fawn
little grrrrrrrr
little house
little ilaw (little ikaw)
little jujube, little journey
little kilay, little kubo
little lumpia
little monster
little night
little opera, little ocean
little phrase, little prairie
little quiet
little rabbit
little starlight, little shout
little tilt, little trace
little universe, little underground
little verve, little volta
little witch, little wonder, little wren
little x
little yodel, little yonder
little zoetrope, little zen

Ingat

I want to give you a world
where knives have no place
save for the mincing of ginger and garlic.
A world where those roots, those bulbs
are talismans we eat
in order for our blood to be strong.

Today, I offer you
the scream I gave to my pillow.
The greying of my mother's hair,
which she gave to me through my phone.
The bread that my friend made
and delivered, which smelled like her home.

I offer you the blooming steam
of my rice cooker.
The bath I've drawn and littered
with salt and kernels of lavender.

May the warm water hold you,
the way a hug might
if I could climb across time
to give it to you.

I QUIT

Babalik Ako

after the work of Ria Unson

we are our own Eden / interior exterior / these moments actually transpired / I dream in English / wrap myself in nostalgia / *foreign in a domestic sense* / are you my ghost sister? / am I my own ghost sister? / I wandered so long / so lonely looking for you / here / you are a portal / portal within a painting / within a portal / internal phenomena / the debts that make these rooms / by luck by chance (if you believe in such things) / we can recover what we've lost / or what was taken / what we never knew / we had homesick I melt into a wall / a house of banana leaves / pothos and orchids / utang na loob an irrecoverable condition / debt and love yakap in transit / babalik ka? / ako rin / take me with you / ako rin

To My Little One (and Their Little One and Their Little One), Long After I Am Gone

*

Not sure you will ever.
Exist survive to read this.
Writing this maybe I will.
You into the future are you.
OK maybe the future has.
Now rewritten over us but.
Here's a dispatch from the past.
We watch the planet rot grow.
Hot burn up dry out flood quake.
A world watching not doing.
Don't know why what could.
You have left after all our prime.
Crime of excess net oceans of.
Plastic histories diluted to forget.
Fulness flavorless poisons we all.
Drink do you have water have you.
Smelled a flower seen a tree a fish.
Your lolo used to collect them.
Small oceans in vast suburbia to.
Remember his first home odds-on.
That's gone now but maybe you're.
Reading this hope you are not.
Totally alone hope you have.
People hope this quaint hope.
You're reading this inside.
An old library full of sunlight.

*

Your lola & lolo loved.
To plant grow harvest.
Soft petal ripe fruit crisp.
Bright leaves seeds our.
Orchids calm sentries.
In bright bay windows.
We were a green thumb.
Family prolific cultivation.
In spaces we could find.
Consent dim basement.
Apartments suburban.
Cul-de-sacs the absolute.
Middle of nowhere growing.
Magic hope your hands are.
Strong like mine the moon.
Of your nails eclipsed.
With dirt is there still.
A garden where I taught.
You how to wait.

*

A truth about our family.
No revolutionaries no.
Rebels a bent neck thin lips.
Talking shit in private might.
Be a family crest if we knew.
Enough to sew it no one learned.
To swim forget making waves.
People said but your people are.
Island people missing the way.
Poverty's a landlocked island.
Maybe you muse how coward.
Ice grows in the blood maybe.
You're judge-y like me due to.
Distance makes everything that.
Came before so easy to run.
Down roast but fears just keep.
Repeating you know the world.
Is round right I hope you've spun.
A bright globe our family made.
Choices cleaved survival to every.
Thing to loudly name worse yet.
To demand anything bahala na.
Bahala ka talaga better to harvest.
Whatever you can hold now.
Can put in your mouth and belly.
Can bank toward some kind.
Of future.

*

Truly we drove one another.
Crazy mother & daughter.
Each generation screaming.
Inside just listen to me plea.
Se conoce alam namin lahat.
Will puncture an expectation.
Toward some better way.
To live too stubborn in all.
The wrong ways all the same.
Knowing the way to love this.
Family has been to never say.
And always be so very sorry.
For all the facts and secrets.
Born before you were ever.
Born into this river of time.
Blood and place hope there.
Is more ease for you hope.
You have found a way.
To learn to forgive us.

SMOOTH PLAINS
LIGHTLY CRATERED PLAINS
MODERATELY CRATERED TERRAIN
CHANNEL AND CANYON DEPOSITS
VOLCANIC CRATERS
VOLCANIC DOMES
VOLCANIC SHIELDS
OLD IMPACT CRATERS
CHAOTIC TERRAIN
GROOVED TERRAIN
FRACTURED PLAINS
GRABENS
(DEPRESSED AREAS BETWEEN FAULT LINES)
200 PCS.
Grand Maitre: Light blue.
Mixed: All colors.
Velvety purple.
Variety
Item #
100
1000
5000
Star Gazer: Vivid red,
edge. Height: 35".
87950
$21.50
$86.00
$345.00
All colors. Height: 35-48"
87953
$20.00
$80.00
$320.00
$39.00
$302.50
$1250.00
87879
$310.00
87877
$310.00
$1280.00
PROFILE, NEXT PAGE
UNITED STATES SUPERIMPOSED TO SCALE
PHOTOGRAPHY MISSING ON MOSAIC ABOVE

*

I wish I could see your face do.
You have my nose I hope you.
Are not scared of the air or hugs.
I hope people don't still blame.
Our faces your face is my face is.
Your Lola's Lola's Lola's pretty.
Strong stock so I think you'll.
Have made it are even maybe.
A singer or scientist or chef or.
Witch that's all in the fam and.
How I know you can hear this.
Hear me from here how I know.
You are still there I am.
Here there with you.

*

There is no one way to.
Love be nimble with your.
Desire love as big as you.
Make it bigger than you think.
When I was little in school.
We played parachute a big.
Rainbow roof made by our.
Arms flapping high and fast.
Until we harnessed enough.
Air to make a new home we.
Used our bodies to anchor.
Our creation we'd sit quiet.
Inside our warm breathing.
Watching our rainbow sink.
Set like a sun become a single.
Blanket I always wanted to.
Live forever inside it sleep.
Then wake there in the.
Snug quiet of our exhales.

*

Food our main language.
We're eaters and feeders.
With rice garlic ginger.
Water and heat you can.
Make a family around.
A steaming pot on a table.
Anywhere you put flowers.
And bowls of food I hope.
You have both hope we.
Have evolved for more.
Laughter and joy to be at.
The center hope we passed.
On some ease some healing.
You'll find me no matter how.
Far time stretches to obscure.
My hair's exact black I love.
You I hope you feel my.
Love like your own pulse I.
Imagine you are well beyond.
All my imaginings exist full-.
Fleshed a hope manifest by.
All the ghosts like me.
Willing you into being.

*

What kind of unimaginable.
Are you have you always.
Loved yourself are you able.
To love others well are your.
Favorite words tikim or bingo.
Do you plait your hair with.
Flowers are you proud are.
You helpful do you cultivate.
Joy do you know I have loved.
You from here always I was.
Once unimaginable nearly.
Unbeholden I tried to write.
A new lexicon sa labas na.
Utang sa lakas ng loob I am.
Not sure if that translates may.
Be your tagalog is better than.
Mine I want you to know.
You owe me nothing only.
Your attempt to be wholly.
Yourself to exist to know my.
Dream for you has always.
Been that you exist brightly.
As full of whatever joy you.
Can create with your own.

*

Know I am still here I.
Speak as if you exist but.
Really I don't know if you'll.
Accept my invitation I do.
Understand why you would.
Not join us here I talk to you.
All of you when I stand at the.
Stove to cook crush garlic with.
The side of my blade I say.
To the you who might never.
Be this is the best way to get.
The most flavor wash rice.
Until all the milky water turns.
Clear close a peace sign let.
Your two fingers rest atop the.
Grains measure the right amount.
Of water the first crease of your.
Hands these are the ways.
We've always said there is love.
All the way from here I am.
We are all rushing toward.
The future to meet you.

.

.

.

ACKNOWLEDGMENTS

Thank you to the editors of the following journals where these poems and collages first appeared.

Bellingham Review: "Hangang Sa Muli," "Little One," and "Stereograph: After A Typhoon—Wherever The Roof Lands, There The Filipino Makes His Home, 1912" / *Hangang Sa Muli* (collage on page 24) and *Wherever The Roof Lands, There The Filipino Makes His Home* (collage on page 34)

Dito Ngayon: A Festschrift for Rofel G. Brion, Perspectives in the Arts & Humanities Asia: "Para Kay Tito Rofel, the First Poet in Our Family"

Frontier Poetry: "I Tell My Mother I Don't Think Getting Pregnant During a Pandemic is a Good Idea"

Georgia Review: "Attempts at Order," "Barangay," "Doppelgänger," "Inspiration," "Just Saying," "This Headline Made Me Think of Being Ten"

Honey Literary: *Haw Flake Lola* (collage on page 62) and *I Quit Lola* (collage on page 71)

Indiana Review:"To My Little One (and their little one and their little one) Long After I Am Gone"

Lantern Review: "How Not to Forget" and "Inside My Lola's Handbag"

Mānoa: A Pacific Journal of International Writing: "Kalilangan," "Kalokohan," "Kalungkutan," "Pagdadalamhati," "Pikon," "Stereograph: The bones of the Tenants . . . , " "Inventory," "Stereograph: 24045 . . . , " "Standardization," and "Failed Self-Portraits"

Memorious: "Why Not End This Experiment?"

New England Review: "Stereograph: School Girl In Native Dress, Upper Garment Made of Hemp Gauze, Philippine Islands, 1907" and "The Captions Are Handwritten"

Northwest Review: "Sight"

Poetry: "All Words I Can Remember Are Poems" and "Utang Na Loob"

Poetry Northwest:"Deals Only We Only Got Deals," "Huwag Kang Matakot," and "Mga Mananaggal Speak" / *Dalanghita Lola* (collage on page 11)

River Styx: "Waves"

Seventh Wave: "Babae," Spawn," "Updates," Q&A," and "Babalik Ako" / *Q&A* / *Ma & Me* (collage on page 77)

Southern Humanities Review: "California" and "Zodiac"

Several texts, authors, scholars, artists, and archives were my guides, companions, and collaborators in the creation of this book. I am indebted to them for inspiring me and informing my research and thinking in the creation of these poems and collages. For a complete bibliography of texts and archives, visit michellepenaloza.com.

"How to Not Forget" is for Ate Susan, Ate Ged, and Ate Gayia. "What You Remember When You And Your Mother Say Miss You Back And Forth On The Phone After Not Having Seen Each Other In Person For Almost Two Years" is indebted to Yona Harvey.

"Kalokohan" is indebted to Catherine and Dot. "Utang Na Loob" is for Jennifer Chang. "Deals Only We Only Got Deals" is for Arlene, Devon, Jane & Tessa. "Q&A" is indebted to Anastacia Rene. "Ingat" is indebted to Rachelle Cruz.

Big, big love to the brilliant and beloved whose friendship and fingerprints have touched this book: Quenton Baker, Bill Carty, Paul Hlava Ceballos, Jennifer Chang, Mike Copperman, Rachelle Cruz, Katherine Limcaoco Diaz, Laurel Flores Fantauzzo, Devon Midori Hale, Ebony Haight, Tessa Hulls, Eddie Kim, Arlene Kim, Janna Añonuevo Langholz, Mita Mahato, Alethea Pace, Anastacia-Reneé, Janice Lobo Sapigao, Matthew Schnirman, Arlo Voorhees, and Jane Wong. Thank you to Willapa Bay AIR and Loghaven for the gift of time and beautiful space to think and work. Tarfia Faizullah, Keetje Kuipers, Barbara Jane Reyes and the Acadamy of American Poets—thank you, thank you for your belief in and support of this book. Deep gratitude to Gabriel Fried and the whole Persea team for their excitement and great care for this book. Maraming yakap and so much love to kapatid Angela Garbes and Jen Soriano for their friendship and their words about this collection. Maraming salamat to all my titas and ates and aunties too numerous to name. Ma, my most opinionated (and loving) muse: laging salamat sa lahat. Alex, my love, thank you for being a true partner in all our endeavors, for being my favorite person, and for always making me feel like I am yours. Dad, Lola, Little One. Thank you for being with me—in this work and always.

And, you, reader. Thank you for reading.

ABOUT THE LEXI RUDNITSKY EDITORS' CHOICE AWARD

The Lexi Rudnitsky Editors' Choice Award is given annually to a poetry collection by a writer who has published at least once previous book of poems. Along with the Lexi Rudnitsky First Book Prize in Poetry, it is a collaboration of Persea Books and the Lexi Rudnitsky Poetry Project. Entry guidelines for both awards are available on Persea's website (www.perseabooks.com).

LEXI RUDNITSKY (1972–2005) grew up outside of Boston, and studied at Brown University and Columbia University. Her own poems exhibit both a playful love of language and a fierce conscience. Her writing appeared in *The Antioch Review, Columbia: A Journal of Literature and Art, The Nation, The New Yorker, The Paris Review, Pequod*, and *The Western Humanities Review*. In 2004, she won the Milton Kessler Memorial Prize for Poetry from *Harpur Palate*.

Lexi died suddenly in 2005, just months after the birth of her first child and the acceptance for publication of her first book of poems, *A Doorless Knocking into Night* (MidList Press, 2006). The Lexi Rudnitsky book prizes were created to memorialize her by promoting the type of poet and poetry in which she so spiritedly believed.

Previous Winners of the Lexi Rudnitsky Editors' Choice Award

2023	Allison Blevins	*Where Will We Live If the House Burns Down?*
2022	Stacie Cassarino	*Each Luminous Thing*
2021	Sarah Carson	*How to Baptize a Child in Flint, Michigan*
2020	Christopher Salerno	*The Man Grave*
2019	Enid Shomer	*Shoreless*
2018	Cameron Awkward-Rich	*Dispatch*
2017	Gary Young	*That's What I Thought*
2016	Heather Derr-Smith	*Thrust*
2015	Shane McCrae	*The Animal Too Big to Kill*
2014	Caki Wilkinson	*The Wynona Stone Poems*
2013	Michael White	*Vermeer in Hell*
2012	Mitchell L. H. Douglas	*/blak/ /al-fə bet/*
2011	Amy Newman	*Dear Editor*